THE POWER *of a* MOTHER

WORDS TO SPEAK AND PRAY
FROM *The Message*

THE POWER *of a* MOTHER

EUGENE H. PETERSON

Bringing Truth to Life

COLORADO SPRINGS, COLORADO

TABLE *of* CONTENTS

Tab. 292.

Kalmia latifolia
Die breitblättrige Kalmie.

I've kept my feet on the ground.

I've cultivated a quiet heart.

Like a baby content in its mother's arms.

my soul is a baby content.

—PSALM 131:2

EXPERIENCE THE POWER
of a MOTHER

❦

There's something so sweet about the bond between mother and child. Remember how many times you ran inside the house with a scraped knee and she was there with a bandage, comforting words, and a big hug? What about the time you rode your bike for the first time without training wheels and she was there at the end of the driveway cheering you on? Then there was your first day of kindergarten. You were nervous as she dressed you up and took a million pictures; she was probably just as nervous, but you never would have known.

Like an open book, you watched me grow from conception to birth;
all the stages of my life were spread out before you,
The days of my life all prepared
before I'd even lived one day. (Psalm 139:16)

Remember that cake she helped you bake for your dad's birthday? There was flour all over the kitchen, and it was a little lopsided, but she was so proud of you! There was your first dance — the dress she helped you pick out, the special shoes she spent too much money on, and the boy she thought wasn't quite good enough for you. Years later she helped you pick out another dress — this one you'd wear to walk down the aisle to the man she knew was perfect for you. Remember the look on her face when you told her she was going to be a grandmother?

> *"When a woman gives birth, she has a hard time, there's no getting around it. But when the baby is born, there is joy in the birth. This new life in the world wipes out memory of the pain." (John 16:21)*

This new life in the world not only wipes out the physical pain of labor but can also clear away the frustration and hurt of not having a mother that was there for you while you were growing up. God has a plan for your life and can redeem your loss. Having kids is almost a second chance at experiencing these scraped knees, lopsided cakes, and first dates.

"Before I shaped you in the womb,
I knew all about you.
Before you saw the light of day,
I had holy plans for you." (Jeremiah 1:5)

We hope that through the pages of this book, you can catch a glimpse of the way God has chosen motherhood as a place of honor: he chose a mother to bring forth humanity, he chose another mother to bring his Son, our savior, into the world, and he chose you to bring life and hope to your kids. So as you read these words, be encouraged, be challenged, and be refreshed. Experience the power of motherhood.

And Mary said,

Yes, I see it all now:
I'm the Lord's maid, ready to serve.
Let it be with me
just as you say. (Luke 1:38)

— THE MESSAGE *Team*

"As a mother comforts her child,

so I'll comfort you.

You will be comforted in Jerusalem."

—ISAIAH 66:13

In Good Company:
Mothers in the Bible

Eve
Genesis 3:20

The Man, known as Adam, named his wife Eve because she
was the mother of all the living.

Genesis 4:1-2

Adam slept with Eve his wife. She conceived and had Cain.
She said, "I've gotten a man, with GOD's help!"

Then she had another baby, Abel. Abel was a herdsman
and Cain a farmer.

SARAH

Genesis 12:1-3, *God's promise for Abram and Sarai*

> GOD told Abram: "Leave your country, your family, and
> your father's home for a land that I will show you.
>
> I'll make you a great nation
>   and bless you.
> I'll make you famous;
>   you'll be a blessing.
> I'll bless those who bless you;
>   those who curse you I'll curse.
> All the families of the Earth
>   will be blessed through you."

Genesis 16:1-11,15-16, *Sarah takes things into her own hands*

> Sarai, Abram's wife, hadn't yet produced a child.
>   She had an Egyptian maid named Hagar. Sarai said to
> Abram, "GOD has not seen fit to let me have a child. Sleep
> with my maid. Maybe I can get a family from her." Abram
> agreed to do what Sarai said.
>   So Sarai, Abram's wife, took her Egyptian maid Hagar

and gave her to her husband Abram as a wife. Abram had been living ten years in Canaan when this took place. He slept with Hagar and she got pregnant. When she learned she was pregnant, she looked down on her mistress.

Sarai told Abram, "It's all your fault that I'm suffering this abuse. I put my maid in bed with you and the minute she knows she's pregnant, she treats me like I'm nothing. May GOD decide which of us is right."

"You decide," said Abram. "Your maid is your business."

Sarai was abusive to Hagar and she ran away.

An angel of GOD found her beside a spring in the desert; it was the spring on the road to Shur. He said, "Hagar, maid of Sarai, what are you doing here?"

She said, "I'm running away from Sarai my mistress."

The angel of GOD said, "Go back to your mistress. Put up with her abuse." He continued, "I'm going to give you a big family, children past counting.

From this pregnancy, you'll get a son: Name him Ishmael; for GOD heard you, GOD answered you." . . .

Hagar gave Abram a son. Abram named him Ishmael. Abram was eighty-six years old when Hagar gave him his son, Ishmael.

Genesis 17:1-5,15-21, *God reminds Abraham of the promise*

When Abram was ninety-nine years old, GOD showed up and said to him, "I am The Strong God, live entirely before me, live to the hilt! I'll make a covenant between us and I'll give you a huge family."

Overwhelmed, Abram fell flat on his face.

Then God said to him, "This is my covenant with you: You'll be the father of many nations. Your name will no longer be Abram, but Abraham, meaning that 'I'm making you the father of many nations.'" . . .

God continued speaking to Abraham, "And Sarai your wife: Don't call her Sarai any longer; call her Sarah. I'll bless her — yes! I'll give you a son by her! Oh, how I'll bless her! Nations will come from her; kings of nations will come from her."

Abraham fell flat on his face. And then he laughed, thinking, "Can a hundred-year-old man father a son? And can Sarah, at ninety years, have a baby?"

Recovering, Abraham said to God, "Oh, keep Ishmael alive and well before you!"

But God said, "That's not what I mean. Your wife, Sarah, will have a baby, a son. Name him Isaac (Laughter). I'll establish my covenant with him and his descendants, a covenant that lasts forever.

"And Ishmael? Yes, I heard your prayer for him. I'll also bless him; I'll make sure he has plenty of children — a huge family. He'll father twelve princes; I'll make him a great nation. But I'll establish my covenant with Isaac whom Sarah will give you about this time next year."

Genesis 18:1-15, *Sarah's doubt*

GOD appeared to Abraham at the Oaks of Mamre while he was sitting at the entrance of his tent. It was the hottest part of the day. He looked up and saw three men standing. He ran from his tent to greet them and bowed before them. He said, "Master, if it please you, stop for a while with your servant. I'll get some water so you can wash your feet. Rest under this tree. I'll get some food to refresh you on your way, since your travels have brought you across my path."

They said, "Certainly. Go ahead."

Abraham hurried into the tent to Sarah. He said, "Hurry. Get three cups of our best flour; knead it and make bread."

Then Abraham ran to the cattle pen and picked out a nice plump calf and gave it to the servant who lost no time getting it ready. Then he got curds and milk, brought them with the calf that had been roasted, set the meal before the men, and stood there under the tree while they ate.

The men said to him, "Where is Sarah your wife?"

He said, "In the tent."

One of them said, "I'm coming back about this time next year. When I arrive, your wife Sarah will have a son." Sarah was listening at the tent opening, just behind the man.

Abraham and Sarah were old by this time, very old. Sarah was far past the age for having babies. Sarah laughed within herself, "An old woman like me? Get pregnant? With this old man of a husband?"

GOD said to Abraham, "Why did Sarah laugh saying, 'Me? Have a baby? An old woman like me?' Is anything too hard for GOD? I'll be back about this time next year and Sarah will have a baby."

Sarah lied. She said, "I didn't laugh," because she was afraid. But he said, "Yes you did; you laughed."

Genesis 21:1-7, *the promise fulfilled*

GOD visited Sarah exactly as he said he would; GOD did to Sarah what he promised: Sarah became pregnant and gave Abraham a son in his old age, and at the very time God had set. Abraham named him Isaac. When his son was eight days old, Abraham circumcised him just as God had commanded.

Abraham was a hundred years old when his son Isaac was born. Sarah said,

God has blessed me with laughter
and all who get the news will laugh with me!

She also said,

Whoever would have suggested to Abraham
that Sarah would one day nurse a baby!
Yet here I am! I've given the old man a son!

Jochebed
Exodus 1:15-22, *a vicious king*

The king of Egypt had a talk with the two Hebrew midwives; one was named Shiphrah and the other Puah. He said, "When you deliver the Hebrew women, look at the sex of the baby. If it's a boy, kill him; if it's a girl, let her live."

But the midwives had far too much respect for God and didn't do what the king of Egypt ordered; they let the boy babies live. The king of Egypt called in the midwives. "Why didn't you obey my orders? You've let those babies live!"

The midwives answered Pharaoh, "The Hebrew women aren't like the Egyptian women; they're vigorous. Before the midwife can get there, they've already had the baby."

God was pleased with the midwives. The people continued to increase in number — a very strong people. And because the midwives honored God, God gave them families of their own.

So Pharaoh issued a general order to all his people: "Every boy that is born, drown him in the Nile. But let the girls live."

Exodus 2:1-10, *a courageous mother*

A man from the family of Levi married a Levite woman. The woman became pregnant and had a son. She saw there was something special about him and hid him. She hid him for three months. When she couldn't hide him any longer she got a little basket-boat made of papyrus, waterproofed it with tar and pitch, and placed the child in it. Then she set it afloat in the reeds at the edge of the Nile.

The baby's older sister found herself a vantage point a little way off and watched to see what would happen to him. Pharaoh's daughter came down to the Nile to bathe; her maidens strolled on the bank. She saw the basket-boat floating in the reeds and sent her maid to get it. She opened it and saw the child — a baby crying! Her heart went out to him. She said, "This must be one of the Hebrew babies."

Then his sister was before her: "Do you want me to go and get a nursing mother from the Hebrews so she can nurse the baby for you?"

Pharaoh's daughter said, "Yes. Go." The girl went and called the child's mother.

Pharaoh's daughter told her, "Take this baby and nurse him for me. I'll pay you." The woman took the child and nursed him.

After the child was weaned, she presented him to Pharaoh's daughter who adopted him as her son. She named him Moses (Pulled-Out), saying, "I pulled him out of the water."

BATHSHEBA
2 Samuel 12:24-25

David went and comforted his wife Bathsheba. And when he slept with her, they conceived a son. When he was born they named him Solomon. GOD had a special love for him and sent word by Nathan the prophet that GOD wanted him named Jedidiah (God's Beloved).

THE SHUNAMMITE WOMAN
2 Kings 4:8-37

One day Elisha passed through Shunem. A leading lady of the town talked him into stopping for a meal. And then it became his custom: Whenever he passed through, he stopped by for a meal.

"I'm certain," said the woman to her husband, "that this man who stops by with us all the time is a holy man of God. Why don't we add on a small room upstairs and furnish it with a bed and desk, chair and lamp, so that when he comes by he can stay with us?"

And so it happened that the next time Elisha came by he went to the room and lay down for a nap.

Then he said to his servant Gehazi, "Tell the Shunammite woman I want to see her." He called her and she came to him.

Through Gehazi Elisha said, "You've gone far beyond the call of duty in taking care of us; what can we do for you? Do you have a request we can bring to the king or to the commander of the army?"

She replied, "Nothing. I'm secure and satisfied in my family."

Elisha conferred with Gehazi: "There's got to be something we can do for her. But what?"

Gehazi said, "Well, she has no son, and her husband is an old man."

"Call her in," said Elisha. He called her and she stood at the open door.

Elisha said to her, "This time next year you're going to be nursing an infant son."

"O my master, O Holy Man," she said, "don't play games with me, teasing me with such fantasies!"

The woman conceived. A year later, just as Elisha had said, she had a son.

The child grew up. One day he went to his father, who was working with the harvest hands, complaining, "My head, my head!"

His father ordered a servant, "Carry him to his mother."

The servant took him in his arms and carried him to his mother. He lay on her lap until noon and died.

She took him up and laid him on the bed of the man of God, shut him in alone, and left.

She then called her husband, "Get me a servant and a donkey so I can go to the Holy Man; I'll be back as soon as I can."

"But why today? This isn't a holy day — it's neither New Moon nor Sabbath."

She said, "Don't ask questions; I need to go right now. Trust me."

She went ahead and saddled the donkey, ordering her

servant, "Take the lead — and go as fast as you can; I'll tell you if you're going too fast." And so off she went. She came to the Holy Man at Mount Carmel.

The Holy Man, spotting her while she was still a long way off, said to his servant Gehazi, "Look out there; why, it's the Shunammite woman! Quickly now. Ask her, 'Is something wrong? Are you all right? Your husband? Your child?'"

She said, "Everything's fine."

But when she reached the Holy Man at the mountain, she threw herself at his feet and held tightly to him.

Gehazi came up to pull her away, but the Holy Man said, "Leave her alone — can't you see that she's in distress? But GOD hasn't let me in on why; I'm completely in the dark."

Then she spoke up: "Did I ask for a son, master? Didn't I tell you, 'Don't tease me with false hopes'?"

He ordered Gehazi, "Don't lose a minute — grab my staff and run as fast as you can. If you meet anyone, don't even take time to greet him, and if anyone greets you, don't even answer. Lay my staff across the boy's face."

The boy's mother said, "As sure as GOD lives and you live, you're not leaving me behind." And so Gehazi let her take the lead, and followed behind.

But Gehazi arrived first and laid the staff across
the boy's face. But there was no sound—no sign of life.
Gehazi went back to meet Elisha and said, "The boy hasn't
stirred."

Elisha entered the house and found the boy
stretched out on the bed dead. He went into the
room and locked the door—just the two of them in
the room—and prayed to GOD. He then got into bed
with the boy and covered him with his body, mouth
on mouth, eyes on eyes, hands on hands. As he was
stretched out over him like that, the boy's body became
warm. Elisha got up and paced back and forth in the
room. Then he went back and stretched himself upon
the boy again. The boy started sneezing—seven times
he sneezed!—and opened his eyes.

He called Gehazi and said, "Get the Shunammite
woman in here!" He called her and she came in.

Elisha said, "Embrace your son!"

She fell at Elisha's feet, face to the ground in reverent
awe. Then she embraced her son and went out with him.

NAOMI

Judges 13:2-5,24, *Samson's mother*

At that time there was a man named Manoah from Zorah from the tribe of Dan. His wife was barren and childless. The angel of God appeared to her and told her, "I know that you are barren and childless, but you're going to become pregnant and bear a son. But take much care: Drink no wine or beer; eat nothing ritually unclean. You are, in fact, pregnant right now, carrying a son. No razor will touch his head — the boy will be God's Nazirite from the moment of his birth. He will launch the deliverance from Philistine oppression." . . .

The woman gave birth to a son. They named him Samson. The boy grew and GOD blessed him.

Ruth 1:1-19

Once upon a time — it was back in the days when judges led Israel — there was a famine in the land. A man from Bethlehem in Judah left home to live in the country of Moab, he and his wife and his two sons. The man's name was Elimelech; his wife's name was Naomi; his sons were named Mahlon and Kilion — all Ephrathites from Bethlehem in Judah. They all went to the country of Moab and settled there.

Elimelech died and Naomi was left, she and her two sons. The sons took Moabite wives; the name of the first was Orpah, the second Ruth. They lived there in Moab for the next ten years. But then the two brothers, Mahlon and Kilion, died. Now the woman was left without either her young men or her husband.

One day she got herself together, she and her two daughters-in-law, to leave the country of Moab and set out for home; she had heard that GOD had been pleased to visit his people and give them food. And so she started out from the place she had been living, she and her two daughters-in-law with her, on the road back to the land of Judah.

After a short while on the road, Naomi told her two daughters-in-law, "Go back. Go home and live with your mothers. And may GOD treat you as graciously as you treated your deceased husbands and me. May GOD give each of you a new home and a new husband!" She kissed them and they cried openly.

They said, "No, we're going on with you to your people."

But Naomi was firm: "Go back, my dear daughters. Why would you come with me? Do you suppose I still have sons in my womb who can become your future husbands? Go back, dear daughters — on your way, please! I'm too old to get a husband. Why, even if I said, 'There's still hope!' and this very night got a man and had sons, can you imagine being satisfied to wait until they were grown? Would you wait that long to get married again? No, dear daughters; this is a bitter pill for me to swallow — more bitter for me than for you. GOD has dealt me a hard blow."

Again they cried openly. Orpah kissed her mother-in-law good-bye; but Ruth embraced her and held on.

Naomi said, "Look, your sister-in-law is going back home to live with her own people and gods; go with her."

But Ruth said, "Don't force me to leave you; don't make me go home. Where you go, I go; and where you live, I'll live. Your people are my people, your God is my god; where you die, I'll die, and that's where I'll be buried, so help me GOD — not even death itself is going to come between us!"

When Naomi saw that Ruth had her heart set on going with her, she gave in. And so the two of them traveled on together to Bethlehem.

WHO IS THE REAL MOTHER?
1 Kings 3:16-27

The very next thing, two prostitutes showed up before the king. The one woman said, "My master, this woman and I live in the same house. While we were living together, I had a baby. Three days after I gave birth, this woman also had a baby. We were alone — there wasn't anyone else in the house except for the two of us. The infant son of this woman died one night when she rolled over on him in her sleep. She got up in the middle of the night and took my son — I was sound asleep, mind you! — and put him at her breast and put her dead son at my breast. When I got up in the morning to nurse my son, here was this dead baby! But when I looked at him in the morning light, I saw immediately that he wasn't my baby."

"Not so!" said the other woman. "The living one's mine; the dead one's yours."

The first woman countered, "No! Your son's the dead one; mine's the living one."

They went back and forth this way in front of the king.

The king said, "What are we to do? This woman says, 'The living son is mine and the dead one is yours,' and this woman says, 'No, the dead one's yours and the living one's mine.'"

After a moment the king said, "Bring me a sword." They brought the sword to the king.

Then he said, "Cut the living baby in two — give half to one and half to the other."

The real mother of the living baby was overcome with emotion for her son and said, "Oh no, master! Give her the whole baby alive; don't kill him!"

But the other one said, "If I can't have him, you can't have him — cut away!"

The king gave his decision: "Give the living baby to the first woman. Nobody is going to kill this baby. She is the real mother."

HANNAH

1 Samuel 1:1-10, *Hannah prays for a child*

There once was a man who lived in Ramathaim. . . . He had two wives. The first was Hannah; the second was Peninnah. Peninnah had children; Hannah did not.

Every year this man went from his hometown up to Shiloh to worship and offer a sacrifice to GOD-of-the-Angel-Armies. Eli and his two sons, Hophni and Phinehas, served as the priests of GOD there. When Elkanah sacrificed, he passed helpings from the sacrificial meal around to his wife Peninnah and all her children, but he always gave an especially generous helping to Hannah because he loved her so much, and because GOD had not given her children. But her rival wife taunted her cruelly, rubbing it in and never letting her forget that GOD had not given her children. This went on year after year. Every time she went to the sanctuary of GOD she could expect to be taunted. Hannah was reduced to tears and had no appetite.

Her husband Elkanah said, "Oh, Hannah, why are you crying? Why aren't you eating? And why are you so upset? Am I not of more worth to you than ten sons?"

So Hannah ate. Then she pulled herself together,

slipped away quietly, and entered the sanctuary. The priest Eli was on duty at the entrance to GOD's Temple in the customary seat. Crushed in soul, Hannah prayed to GOD and cried and cried — inconsolably.

1 Samuel 1:11-18, *Hannah's vow*

Then she made a vow:

> Oh, GOD-of-the-Angel-Armies,
> If you'll take a good, hard look at my pain,
> If you'll quit neglecting me and go into action for me
> By giving me a son,
> I'll give him completely, unreservedly to you.
> I'll set him apart for a life of holy discipline.

It so happened that as she continued in prayer before GOD, Eli was watching her closely. Hannah was praying in her heart, silently. Her lips moved, but no sound was heard. Eli jumped to the conclusion that she was drunk. He approached her and said, "You're drunk! How long do you plan to keep this up? Sober up, woman!"

Hannah said, "Oh no, sir — please! I'm a woman hard

used. I haven't been drinking. Not a drop of wine or beer. The only thing I've been pouring out is my heart, pouring it out to GOD. Don't for a minute think I'm a bad woman. It's because I'm so desperately unhappy and in such pain that I've stayed here so long."

Eli answered her, "Go in peace. And may the God of Israel give you what you have asked of him."

"Think well of me — and pray for me!" she said, and went her way. Then she ate heartily, her face radiant.

1 Samuel 1:19-28, *Hannah's prayer is answered*

Up before dawn, they worshiped GOD and returned home to Ramah. Elkanah slept with Hannah his wife, and GOD began making the necessary arrangements in response to what she had asked.

Before the year was out, Hannah had conceived and given birth to a son. She named him Samuel, explaining, "I asked GOD for him."

When Elkanah next took his family on their annual trip to Shiloh to worship GOD, offering sacrifices and keeping his vow, Hannah didn't go. She told her husband, "After the child is weaned, I'll bring him myself and present him before GOD — and that's where he'll stay, for good."

Elkanah said to his wife, "Do what you think is best. Stay home until you have weaned him. Yes! Let GOD complete what he has begun!"

So she did. She stayed home and nursed her son until she had weaned him. Then she took him up to Shiloh, bringing also the makings of a generous sacrificial meal — a prize bull, flour, and wine. The child was so young to be sent off!

They first butchered the bull, then brought the child to Eli. Hannah said, "Excuse me, sir. Would you believe that I'm the very woman who was standing before you at this very spot, praying to GOD? I prayed for this child, and GOD gave me what I asked for. And now I have dedicated him to GOD. He's dedicated to GOD for life."

Then and there, they worshiped GOD.

1 Samuel 2:1-10, *Hannah's praise*

Hannah prayed:

I'm bursting with God-news!
    I'm walking on air.

I'm laughing at my rivals.

I'm dancing my salvation.

Nothing and no one is holy like GOD,

no rock mountain like our God.

Don't dare talk pretentiously —

not a word of boasting, ever!

For GOD knows what's going on.

He takes the measure of everything that happens.

The weapons of the strong are smashed to pieces,

while the weak are infused with fresh strength.

The well-fed are out begging in the streets for crusts,

while the hungry are getting second helpings.

The barren woman has a houseful of children,

while the mother of many is bereft.

GOD brings death and GOD brings life,

brings down to the grave and raises up.

GOD brings poverty and GOD brings wealth;

he lowers, he also lifts up.

He puts poor people on their feet again;

he rekindles burned-out lives with fresh hope,

Restoring dignity and respect to their lives—

    a place in the sun!

For the very structures of earth are GOD's;

    he has laid out his operations on a firm foundation.

He protectively cares for his faithful friends, step by step,

    but leaves the wicked to stumble in the dark.

    No one makes it in this life by sheer muscle!

GOD's enemies will be blasted out of the sky,

    crashed in a heap and burned.

GOD will set things right all over the earth,

    he'll give strength to his king,

    he'll set his anointed on top of the world!

1 Samuel 2:11,18-21, *God's kindness for Hannah*

Elkanah went home to Ramah. The boy stayed and served GOD in the company of Eli the priest. . . .

In the midst of all this, Samuel, a boy dressed in a priestly linen tunic, served GOD. Additionally, every year his mother would make him a little robe cut to his size and bring it to him when she and her husband came for the annual sacrifice. Eli would bless Elkanah and his wife, saying, "GOD give you children to replace this child you have dedicated to GOD." Then they would go home.

GOD was most especially kind to Hannah. She had three more sons and two daughters! The boy Samuel stayed at the sanctuary and grew up with GOD.

ELIZABETH

Luke 1:5-20,24, *Elizabeth's pregnancy announced by an angel*

During the rule of Herod, King of Judea, there was a priest assigned service in the regiment of Abijah. His name was Zachariah. His wife was descended from the daughters of Aaron. Her name was Elizabeth. Together they lived honorably before God, careful in keeping to the ways of the commandments and enjoying a clear conscience before God. But they were childless because Elizabeth could never conceive, and now they were quite old.

It so happened that as Zachariah was carrying out his priestly duties before God, working the shift assigned to his regiment, it came his one turn in life to enter the sanctuary of God and burn incense. The congregation was gathered and praying outside the Temple at the hour of the incense offering. Unannounced, an angel of God appeared just to the right of the altar of incense. Zachariah was paralyzed in fear.

But the angel reassured him, "Don't fear, Zachariah. Your prayer has been heard. Elizabeth, your wife, will bear a son by you. You are to name him John. You're going to leap like a gazelle for joy, and not only you — many will delight in his birth. He'll achieve great stature with God.

"He'll drink neither wine nor beer. He'll be filled with the Holy Spirit from the moment he leaves his mother's womb. He will turn many sons and daughters of Israel back to their God. He will herald God's arrival in the style and strength of Elijah, soften the hearts of parents to children, and kindle devout understanding among hardened skeptics — he'll get the people ready for God."

Zachariah said to the angel, "Do you expect me to believe this? I'm an old man and my wife is an old woman."

But the angel said, "I am Gabriel, the sentinel of God, sent especially to bring you this glad news. But because you won't believe me, you'll be unable to say a word until the day of your son's birth. Every word I've spoken to you will come true on time — *God's* time." . . .

It wasn't long before his wife, Elizabeth, conceived. She went off by herself for five months, relishing her pregnancy.

MARY

Luke 1:26-38, *Mary conceives*

In the sixth month of Elizabeth's pregnancy, God sent the angel Gabriel to the Galilean village of Nazareth to a virgin engaged to be married to a man descended from David. His name was Joseph, and the virgin's name, Mary. Upon entering, Gabriel greeted her:

Good morning!
You're beautiful with God's beauty,
Beautiful inside and out!
God be with you.

She was thoroughly shaken, wondering what was behind a greeting like that. But the angel assured her, "Mary, you have nothing to fear. God has a surprise for you: You will become pregnant and give birth to a son and call his name Jesus.

He will be great,
be called 'Son of the Highest.'
The Lord God will give him
the throne of his father David;

He will rule Jacob's house forever—
    no end, ever, to his kingdom."

Mary said to the angel, "But how? I've never slept with
    a man."
The angel answered,

The Holy Spirit will come upon you,
    the power of the Highest hover over you;
Therefore, the child you bring to birth
    will be called Holy, Son of God.

"And did you know that your cousin Elizabeth conceived a son, old as she is? Everyone called her barren, and
here she is six months pregnant! Nothing, you see, is impos-
sible with God."
And Mary said,

Yes, I see it all now:
    I'm the Lord's maid, ready to serve.
Let it be with me
    just as you say.

Then the angel left her.

Matthew 1:18-25, *Mary's pregnancy*

The birth of Jesus took place like this. His mother, Mary, was engaged to be married to Joseph. Before they came to the marriage bed, Joseph discovered she was pregnant. (It was by the Holy Spirit, but he didn't know that.) Joseph, chagrined but noble, determined to take care of things quietly so Mary would not be disgraced.

While he was trying to figure a way out, he had a dream. God's angel spoke in the dream: "Joseph, son of David, don't hesitate to get married. Mary's pregnancy is Spirit-conceived. God's Holy Spirit has made her pregnant. She will bring a son to birth, and when she does, you, Joseph, will name him Jesus — 'God saves' — because he will save his people from their sins." This would bring the prophet's embryonic sermon to full term:

Watch for this—a virgin will get pregnant and bear a son;
They will name him Emmanuel (Hebrew for "God is
    with us").

Then Joseph woke up. He did exactly what God's angel commanded in the dream: He married Mary. But he did not consummate the marriage until she had the baby. He named the baby Jesus.

ELIZABETH AND MARY
Luke 1:39-45, *Elizabeth and Mary rejoice*

Mary didn't waste a minute. She got up and traveled to a town in Judah in the hill country, straight to Zachariah's house, and greeted Elizabeth. When Elizabeth heard Mary's greeting, the baby in her womb leaped. She was filled with the Holy Spirit, and sang out exuberantly,

You're so blessed among women,
    and the babe in your womb, also blessed!
And why am I so blessed that
    the mother of my Lord visits me?
The moment the sound of your
    greeting entered my ears,
The babe in my womb
    skipped like a lamb for sheer joy.
Blessed woman, who believed what God said,
    believed every word would come true!

MARY

Luke 1:46-55, *Mary's joy*

And Mary said,

I'm bursting with God-news;
    I'm dancing the song of my Savior God.
God took one good look at me, and look what happened —
    I'm the most fortunate woman on earth!
What God has done for me will never be forgotten,
    the God whose very name is holy, set apart from all
        others.
His mercy flows in wave after wave
    on those who are in awe before him.
He bared his arm and showed his strength,
    scattered the bluffing braggarts.
He knocked tyrants off their high horses,
    pulled victims out of the mud.
The starving poor sat down to a banquet;
    the callous rich were left out in the cold.
He embraced his chosen child, Israel;
    he remembered and piled on the mercies, piled
        them high.

It's exactly what he promised,
>   beginning with Abraham and right up to now.

Elizabeth
Luke 1:57-66, *Elizabeth has a son*

When Elizabeth was full-term in her pregnancy, she bore a son. Her neighbors and relatives, seeing that God had overwhelmed her with mercy, celebrated with her.

On the eighth day, they came to circumcise the child and were calling him Zachariah after his father. But his mother intervened: "No. He is to be called John."

"But," they said, "no one in your family is named that." They used sign language to ask Zachariah what he wanted him named.

Asking for a tablet, Zachariah wrote, "His name is to be John." That took everyone by surprise. Surprise followed surprise — Zachariah's mouth was now open, his tongue loose, and he was talking, praising God!

A deep, reverential fear settled over the neighborhood, and in all that Judean hill country people talked about nothing else. Everyone who heard about it took it to heart, wondering, "What will become of this child? Clearly, God has his hand in this."

MARY

Luke 2:41-52, *Mary as Jesus grows*

Every year Jesus' parents traveled to Jerusalem for the Feast of Passover. When he was twelve years old, they went up as they always did for the Feast. When it was over and they left for home, the child Jesus stayed behind in Jerusalem, but his parents didn't know it. Thinking he was somewhere in the company of pilgrims, they journeyed for a whole day and then began looking for him among relatives and neighbors. When they didn't find him, they went back to Jerusalem looking for him.

The next day they found him in the Temple seated among the teachers, listening to them and asking questions. The teachers were all quite taken with him, impressed with the sharpness of his answers. But his parents were not impressed; they were upset and hurt.

His mother said, "Young man, why have you done this to us? Your father and I have been half out of our minds looking for you."

He said, "Why were you looking for me? Didn't you know that I had to be here, dealing with the things of my Father?" But they had no idea what he was talking about.

So he went back to Nazareth with them, and lived obediently with them. His mother held these things dearly, deep within herself. And Jesus matured, growing up in both body and spirit, blessed by both God and people.

James and John's Mother
Matthew 20:20-23

It was about that time that the mother of the Zebedee brothers came with her two sons and knelt before Jesus with a request.

"What do you want?" Jesus asked.

She said, "Give your word that these two sons of mine will be awarded the highest places of honor in your kingdom, one at your right hand, one at your left hand."

Jesus responded, "You have no idea what you're asking." And he said to James and John, "Are you capable of drinking the cup that I'm about to drink?"

They said, "Sure, why not?"

Jesus said, "Come to think of it, you *are* going to drink my cup. But as to awarding places of honor, that's not my business. My Father is taking care of that."

Mary
John 19:16-18,25-27, *a mother's loss*

> They took Jesus away. Carrying his cross, Jesus went out to the place called Skull Hill (the name in Hebrew is *Golgotha*), where they crucified him, and with him two others, one on each side, Jesus in the middle. . . .
>
> Jesus' mother, his aunt, Mary the wife of Clopas, and Mary Magdalene stood at the foot of the cross. Jesus saw his mother and the disciple he loved standing near her. He said to his mother, "Woman, here is your son." Then to the disciple, "Here is your mother." From that moment the disciple accepted her as his own mother.

Oh yes, you shaped me first inside, then out;

you formed me in my mother's womb.

I thank you, High God—you're breathtaking!

Body and soul, I am marvelously made!

I worship in adoration—what a creation!

You know me inside and out,

you know every bone in my body;

You know exactly how I was made, bit by bit,

how I was sculpted from nothing into something.

—Psalm 139:13-15

Mary, you have nothing to fear. God has a surprise for you: You will become pregnant and give birth to a son and call his name Jesus.

—LUKE 1:30-31

GOD'S INSTRUCTION

❧

Proverbs 14:26

> The Fear-of-GOD builds up confidence,
>   and makes a world safe for your children.

Deuteronomy 11:18-20

> Place these words on your hearts. Get them deep inside you.
> Tie them on your hands and foreheads as a reminder. Teach
> them to your children. Talk about them wherever you are,
> sitting at home or walking in the street; talk about them
> from the time you get up in the morning until you fall into
> bed at night. Inscribe them on the doorposts and gates of
> your cities.

Deuteronomy 12:28

> Be vigilant, listen obediently to these words that I command you so that you'll have a good life, you and your children, for a long, long time, doing what is good and right in the eyes of GOD, your God.

Proverbs 22:6

> Point your kids in the right direction —
> when they're old they won't be lost.

Ephesians 6:4

> Don't exasperate your children by coming down hard on them. Take them by the hand and lead them in the way of the Master.

Proverbs 29:17

> Discipline your children; you'll be glad you did —
> they'll turn out delightful to live with.

Proverbs 23:13-14

> Don't be afraid to correct your young ones;
>   a spanking won't kill them.
> A good spanking, in fact, might save them
>   from something worse than death.

Deuteronomy 6:1-2

> This is the commandment, the rules and regulations, that
> GOD, your God, commanded me to teach you to live out in
> the land you're about to cross into to possess. This is so that
> you'll live in deep reverence before GOD lifelong, observing
> all his rules and regulations that I'm commanding you, you
> and your children and your grandchildren, living good long
> lives.

Proverbs 19:18

> Discipline your children while you still have the chance;
>   indulging them destroys them.

Proverbs 29:15

> Wise discipline imparts wisdom;
>> spoiled adolescents embarrass their parents.

Deuteronomy 4:9

> Just make sure you stay alert. Keep close watch over your-
> selves. Don't forget anything of what you've seen. Don't
> let your heart wander off. Stay vigilant as long as you live.
> Teach what you've seen and heard to your children and
> grandchildren.

Colossians 3:21

> Parents, don't come down too hard on your children or
> you'll crush their spirits.

Proverbs 13:24

> A refusal to correct is a refusal to love;
>> love your children by disciplining them.

Titus 2:3-5

> Guide older women into lives of reverence so they end up as neither gossips nor drunks, but models of goodness. By looking at them, the younger women will know how to love their husbands and children, be virtuous and pure, keep a good house, be good wives.

1 Corinthians 14:26

> So here's what I want you to do. When you gather for worship, each one of you be prepared with something that will be useful for all: Sing a hymn, teach a lesson, tell a story, lead a prayer, provide an insight.

Deuteronomy 6:6-7

> Write these commandments that I've given you today on your hearts. Get them inside of you and then get them inside your children. Talk about them wherever you are, sitting at home or walking in the street; talk about them from the time you get up in the morning to when you fall into bed at night.

Deuteronomy 6:20-25

The next time your child asks you, "What do these require-
ments and regulations and rules that GOD, our God, has
commanded mean?" tell your child, "We were slaves to
Pharaoh in Egypt and GOD powerfully intervened and got
us out of that country. We stood there and watched as GOD
delivered miracle-signs, great wonders, and evil-visitations
on Egypt, on Pharaoh and his household. He pulled us out
of there so he could bring us here and give us the land he so
solemnly promised to our ancestors. That's why GOD commanded us to follow all these rules, so that we would live
reverently before GOD, our God, as he gives us this good
life, keeping us alive for a long time to come.

"It will be a set-right and put-together life for us if
we make sure that we do this entire commandment in the
Presence of GOD, our God, just as he commanded us to do."

Jesus saw his mother and the disciple he loved standing near her.

He said to his mother, "Woman, here is your son."

—JOHN 19:26

Point your kids in the right direction—

when they're old they won't be lost.

— PROVERBS 22:6

MOTHERLY ADVICE

1 Peter 3:3-4

What matters is not your outer appearance — the styling of
your hair, the jewelry you wear, the cut of your clothes — but
your inner disposition.

Cultivate inner beauty, the gentle, gracious kind that
God delights in.

Colossians 3:12-14

So, chosen by God for this new life of love, dress in the
wardrobe God picked out for you: compassion, kindness,
humility, quiet strength, discipline. Be even-tempered, content with second place, quick to forgive an offense. Forgive
as quickly and completely as the Master forgave you. And

regardless of what else you put on, wear love. It's your basic, all-purpose garment. Never be without it.

Galatians 6:7-9

Don't be misled: No one makes a fool of God. What a person plants, he will harvest. The person who plants selfishness, ignoring the needs of others — ignoring God! — harvests a crop of weeds. All he'll have to show for his life is weeds! But the one who plants in response to God, letting God's Spirit do the growth work in him, harvests a crop of real life, eternal life.

So let's not allow ourselves to get fatigued doing good. At the right time we will harvest a good crop if we don't give up, or quit.

Proverbs 6:20-23

Good friend, follow your father's good advice;
    don't wander off from your mother's teachings.
Wrap yourself in them from head to foot;
    wear them like a scarf around your neck.
Wherever you walk, they'll guide you;

whenever you rest, they'll guard you;
>   when you wake up, they'll tell you what's next.
For sound advice is a beacon,
>   good teaching is a light,
>   moral discipline is a life path.

1 Corinthians 6:12

Just because something is technically legal doesn't mean
that it's spiritually appropriate. If I went around doing
whatever I thought I could get by with, I'd be a slave to my
whims.

Psalm 119:9-11

How can a young person live a clean life?
>   By carefully reading the map of your Word.
I'm single-minded in pursuit of you;
>   don't let me miss the road signs you've posted.
I've banked your promises in the vault of my heart
>   so I won't sin myself bankrupt.

Proverbs 15:25-33

GOD smashes the pretensions of the arrogant;
    he stands with those who have no standing.

GOD can't stand evil scheming,
    but he puts words of grace and beauty on display.

A greedy and grasping person destroys community;
    those who refuse to exploit live and let live.

Prayerful answers come from God-loyal people;
    the wicked are sewers of abuse.

GOD keeps his distance from the wicked;
    he closely attends to the prayers of God-loyal people.

A twinkle in the eye means joy in the heart,
    and good news makes you feel fit as a fiddle.

Listen to good advice if you want to live well,
    an honored guest among wise men and women.

An undisciplined, self-willed life is puny;
    an obedient, God-willed life is spacious.

Fear-of-GOD is a school in skilled living—
    first you learn humility, then you experience glory.

Ephesians 4:32

    Be gentle with one another, sensitive. Forgive one another
    as quickly and thoroughly as God in Christ forgave you.

Matthew 6:14-15

    "In prayer there is a connection between what God does
    and what you do. You can't get forgiveness from God, for
    instance, without also forgiving others. If you refuse to do
    your part, you cut yourself off from God's part."

Psalm 32:8-10

    Let me give you some good advice;
        I'm looking you in the eye
        and giving it to you straight:

"Don't be ornery like a horse or mule
    that needs bit and bridle
    to stay on track."

God-defiers are always in trouble;
    GOD-affirmers find themselves loved
    every time they turn around.

Proverbs 1:7

Start with GOD—the first step in learning is bowing down
        to GOD;
        only fools thumb their noses at such wisdom and learning.

James 3:13-18

Do you want to be counted wise, to build a reputation for
wisdom? Here's what you do: Live well, live wisely, live
humbly. It's the way you live, not the way you talk, that
counts. Mean-spirited ambition isn't wisdom. Boasting
that you are wise isn't wisdom. Twisting the truth to make
yourselves sound wise isn't wisdom. It's the furthest thing
from wisdom — it's animal cunning, devilish conniving.

Whenever you're trying to look better than others or get
the better of others, things fall apart and everyone ends up
at the others' throats.

Real wisdom, God's wisdom, begins with a holy life and
is characterized by getting along with others. It is gentle
and reasonable, overflowing with mercy and blessings, not
hot one day and cold the next, not two-faced. You can
develop a healthy, robust community that lives right with
God and enjoy its results *only* if you do the hard work of
getting along with each other, treating each other with dignity and honor.

Proverbs 1:8-9

Pay close attention, friend, to what your father tells you;
    never forget what you learned at your mother's knee.
Wear their counsel like flowers in your hair,
    like rings on your fingers.

Romans 8:26-28

Meanwhile, the moment we get tired in the waiting, God's
Spirit is right alongside helping us along. If we don't know

how or what to pray, it doesn't matter. He does our praying in and for us, making prayer out of our wordless sighs, our aching groans. He knows us far better than we know our-selves, knows our pregnant condition, and keeps us present before God. That's why we can be so sure that every detail in our lives of love for God is worked into something good.

Philippians 4:6-7

Don't fret or worry. Instead of worrying, pray. Let petitions and praises shape your worries into prayers, letting God know your concerns. Before you know it, a sense of God's wholeness, everything coming together for good, will come and settle you down. It's wonderful what happens when Christ displaces worry at the center of your life.

2 Corinthians 9:6-7

Remember: A stingy planter gets a stingy crop; a lavish planter gets a lavish crop. I want each of you to take plenty of time to think it over, and make up your own mind what you will give. That will protect you against sob stories and arm-twisting. God loves it when the giver delights in the giving.

Proverbs 16:32

> Moderation is better than muscle,
>> self-control better than political power.

Proverbs 12:25

> Worry weighs us down;
>> a cheerful word picks us up.

Hebrews 13:1-8

> Stay on good terms with each other, held together by love.
> Be ready with a meal or a bed when it's needed. Why, some
> have extended hospitality to angels without ever knowing
> it! Regard prisoners as if you were in prison with them.
> Look on victims of abuse as if what happened to them had
> happened to you. Honor marriage, and guard the sacredness
> of sexual intimacy between wife and husband. God draws a
> firm line against casual and illicit sex.
>
> Don't be obsessed with getting more material things.
> Be relaxed with what you have. Since God assured us, "I'll
> never let you down, never walk off and leave you," we can
> boldly quote,

God is there, ready to help;
I'm fearless no matter what.
Who or what can get to me?

Appreciate your pastoral leaders who gave you the
Word of God. Take a good look at the way they live, and
let their faithfulness instruct you, as well as their truthful-
ness. There should be a consistency that runs through us all.
For Jesus doesn't change — yesterday, today, tomorrow, he's
always totally himself.

Proverbs 18:20-21

Words satisfy the mind as much as fruit does the stomach;
    good talk is as gratifying as a good harvest.

Words kill, words give life;
    they're either poison or fruit — you choose.

Psalm 138:8

Finish what you started in me, GOD.
    Your love is eternal — don't quit on me now.

Proverbs 31:1-9

The words of King Lemuel,
    the strong advice his mother gave him:

"Oh, son of mine, what can you be thinking of!
    Child whom I bore! The son I dedicated to God!
Don't dissipate your virility on fortune-hunting women,
    promiscuous women who shipwreck leaders.

"Leaders can't afford to make fools of themselves,
    gulping wine and swilling beer,
Lest, hung over, they don't know right from wrong,
    and the people who depend on them are hurt.
Use wine and beer only as sedatives,
    to kill the pain and dull the ache
Of the terminally ill,
    for whom life is a living death.

"Speak up for the people who have no voice,
    for the rights of all the down-and-outers.
Speak out for justice!
    Stand up for the poor and destitute!"

Proverbs 17:22

> A cheerful disposition is good for your health;
>> gloom and doom leave you bone-tired.

James 4:7-10

> So let God work his will in you. Yell a loud *no* to the Devil
> and watch him scamper. Say a quiet *yes* to God and he'll be
> there in no time. Quit dabbling in sin. Purify your inner
> life. Quit playing the field. Hit bottom, and cry your eyes
> out. The fun and games are over. Get serious, really serious.
> Get down on your knees before the Master; it's the only
> way you'll get on your feet.

2 Peter 3:8-9

> Don't overlook the obvious here, friends. With God, one
> day is as good as a thousand years, a thousand years as a day.
> God isn't late with his promise as some measure lateness.
> He is restraining himself on account of you, holding back
> the End because he doesn't want anyone lost. He's giving
> everyone space and time to change.

Philippians 1:6

There has never been the slightest doubt in my mind that the God who started this great work in you would keep at it and bring it to a flourishing finish on the very day Christ Jesus appears.

Hibiscus syriacus flore variegato.
Der syrische Hibischstrauch mit fleckiger Blüthe.

"All your children will have GOD

for their teacher —

what a mentor for your children!"

—ISAIAH 54:13

THE LEGACY *of a* MOTHER

Joel 1:3

Make sure you tell your children,
    and your children tell their children,
And their children *their* children.
    Don't let this message die out.

Acts 2:38-39

Peter said, "Change your life. Turn to God and be baptized,
each of you, in the name of Jesus Christ, so your sins are
forgiven. Receive the gift of the Holy Spirit. The promise is
targeted to you and your children, but also to all who are far
away — whomever, in fact, our Master God invites."

2 Timothy 3:14-15

> Stick with what you learned and believed, sure of the
> integrity of your teachers — why, you took in the sacred
> Scriptures with your mother's milk! There's nothing like
> the written Word of God for showing you the way to salva-
> tion through faith in Christ Jesus.

Philippians 1:6

> There has never been the slightest doubt in my mind that
> the God who started this great work in you would keep at
> it and bring it to a flourishing finish on the very day Christ
> Jesus appears.

Romans 9:28-29

> God doesn't count us; he calls us by name.
> Arithmetic is not his focus.
>
> Isaiah had looked ahead and spoken the truth:
> If our powerful God
> had not provided us a legacy of living children,

We would have ended up like ghost towns,
 like Sodom and Gomorrah.

2 Timothy 1:5

That precious memory triggers another: your honest
faith — and what a rich faith it is, handed down from your
grandmother Lois to your mother Eunice, and now to you!

Psalm 127:3-5

Don't you see that children are GOD's best gift?
 the fruit of the womb his generous legacy?
Like a warrior's fistful of arrows
 are the children of a vigorous youth.
Oh, how blessed are you parents,
 with your quivers full of children!
Your enemies don't stand a chance against you;
 you'll sweep them right off your doorstep

Psalm 112:1-3

> Hallelujah!
> Blessed man, blessed woman, who fear GOD,
> Who cherish and relish his commandments,
> Their children robust on the earth,
> And the homes of the upright — how blessed!
> Their houses brim with wealth
> And a generosity that never runs dry.

Your love, GOD, is my song, and I'll sing it!
I'm forever telling everyone how faithful you are.
I'll never quit telling the story of your love—
how you built the cosmos
and guaranteed everything in it.
Your love has always been our lives' foundation,
your fidelity has been the roof over our world.

—PSALM 89:1-2

If Abraham, by what he did for God,

got God to approve him, he could certainly

have taken credit for it. But the story

we're given is a God-story, not an Abraham-story.

—ROMANS 4:2

STORIES WITH A LESSON TO SHARE WITH YOUR KIDS

❧

Matthew 13:3-9,18-23, *the story of a harvest*

"What do you make of this? A farmer planted seed. As he scattered the seed, some of it fell on the road, and birds ate it. Some fell in the gravel; it sprouted quickly but didn't put down roots, so when the sun came up it withered just as quickly. Some fell in the weeds; as it came up, it was strangled by the weeds. Some fell on good earth, and produced a harvest beyond his wildest dreams.

"Are you listening to this? Really listening?" . . .

"Study this story of the farmer planting seed. When anyone hears news of the kingdom and doesn't take it in, it just remains on the surface, and so the Evil One comes along and plucks it right out of that person's heart. This is the seed the farmer scatters on the road.

"The seed cast in the gravel — this is the person who hears and instantly responds with enthusiasm. But there is no soil of character, and so when the emotions wear off and some difficulty arrives, there is nothing to show for it.

"The seed cast in the weeds is the person who hears the kingdom news, but weeds of worry and illusions about getting more and wanting everything under the sun strangle what was heard, and nothing comes of it.

"The seed cast on good earth is the person who hears and takes in the News, and then produces a harvest beyond his wildest dreams."

Matthew 13:24-30,36-44, *the story of God's kingdom*

He told another story. "God's kingdom is like a farmer who planted good seed in his field. That night, while his hired men were asleep, his enemy sowed thistles all through the wheat and slipped away before dawn. When the first green shoots appeared and the grain began to form, the thistles showed up, too.

"The farmhands came to the farmer and said, 'Master, that was clean seed you planted, wasn't it? Where did these thistles come from?'

"He answered, 'Some enemy did this.'

"The farmhands asked, 'Should we weed out the thistles?'

"He said, 'No, if you weed the thistles, you'll pull up the wheat, too. Let them grow together until harvest time. Then I'll instruct the harvesters to pull up the thistles and tie them in bundles for the fire, then gather the wheat and put it in the barn.'" . . .

Jesus dismissed the congregation and went into the house. His disciples came in and said, "Explain to us that story of the thistles in the field."

So he explained. "The farmer who sows the pure seed is the Son of Man. The field is the world, the pure seeds are subjects of the kingdom, the thistles are subjects of the Devil, and the enemy who sows them is the Devil. The harvest is the end of the age, the curtain of history. The harvest hands are angels.

"The picture of thistles pulled up and burned is a scene from the final act. The Son of Man will send his angels, weed out the thistles from his kingdom, pitch them in the trash, and be done with them. They are going to complain to high heaven, but nobody is going to listen. At the same time, ripe, holy lives will mature and adorn the kingdom of their Father.

"Are you listening to this? Really listening?

"God's kingdom is like a treasure hidden in a field for years and then accidently found by a trespasser. The finder is ecstatic — what a find! — and proceeds to sell everything he owns to raise money and buy that field."

Matthew 21:28-32, *the story of two sons*

"Tell me what you think of this story: A man had two sons. He went up to the first and said, 'Son, go out for the day and work in the vineyard.'

"The son answered, 'I don't want to.' Later on he thought better of it and went.

"The father gave the same command to the second son. He answered, 'Sure, glad to.' But he never went.

"Which of the two sons did what the father asked?"

They said, "The first."

Jesus said, "Yes, and I tell you that crooks and whores are going to precede you into God's kingdom. John came to you showing you the right road. You turned up your noses at him, but the crooks and whores believed him. Even when you saw their changed lives, you didn't care enough to change and believe him."

Matthew 21:33-44, *the story of the greedy farmhands*

"Here's another story. Listen closely. There was once a man, a wealthy farmer, who planted a vineyard. He fenced it, dug a winepress, put up a watchtower, then turned it over to the farmhands and went off on a trip. When it was time to harvest the grapes, he sent his servants back to collect his profits.

"The farmhands grabbed the first servant and beat him up. The next one they murdered. They threw stones at the third but he got away. The owner tried again, sending more servants. They got the same treatment. The owner was at the end of his rope. He decided to send his son. 'Surely,' he thought, 'they will respect my son.'

"But when the farmhands saw the son arrive, they rubbed their hands in greed. 'This is the heir! Let's kill him and have it all for ourselves.' They grabbed him, threw him out, and killed him.

"Now, when the owner of the vineyard arrives home from his trip, what do you think he will do to the farm-hands?"

"He'll kill them — a rotten bunch, and good riddance," they answered. "Then he'll assign the vineyard to farm-hands who will hand over the profits when it's time."

Jesus said, "Right — and you can read it for yourselves in your Bibles:

The stone the masons threw out
is now the cornerstone.
This is God's work;
we rub our eyes, we can hardly believe it!

"This is the way it is with you. God's kingdom will be taken back from you and handed over to a people who will live out a kingdom life. Whoever stumbles on this Stone gets shattered; whoever the Stone falls on gets smashed."

Matthew 22:1-14, *the story of the wedding banquet*

Jesus responded by telling still more stories. "God's kingdom," he said, "is like a king who threw a wedding banquet for his son. He sent out servants to call in all the invited guests. And they wouldn't come!

"He sent out another round of servants, instructing

them to tell the guests, 'Look, everything is on the table, the prime rib is ready for carving. Come to the feast!'

"They only shrugged their shoulders and went off, one to weed his garden, another to work in his shop. The rest, with nothing better to do, beat up on the messengers and then killed them. The king was outraged and sent his soldiers to destroy those thugs and level their city.

"Then he told his servants, 'We have a wedding banquet all prepared but no guests. The ones I invited weren't up to it. Go out into the busiest intersections in town and invite anyone you find to the banquet.' The servants went out on the streets and rounded up everyone they laid eyes on, good and bad, regardless. And so the banquet was on — every place filled.

"When the king entered and looked over the scene, he spotted a man who wasn't properly dressed. He said to him, 'Friend, how dare you come in here looking like that!' The man was speechless. Then the king told his servants, 'Get him out of here — fast. Tie him up and ship him to hell. And make sure he doesn't get back in.'

"That's what I mean when I say, 'Many get invited; only a few make it.'"

Matthew 25:14-30, *the story about investment*

"It's also like a man going off on an extended trip. He called his servants together and delegated responsibilities. To one he gave five thousand dollars, to another two thousand, to a third one thousand, depending on their abilities. Then he left. Right off, the first servant went to work and doubled his master's investment. The second did the same. But the man with the single thousand dug a hole and carefully buried his master's money.

"After a long absence, the master of those three servants came back and settled up with them. The one given five thousand dollars showed him how he had doubled his investment. His master commended him: 'Good work! You did your job well. From now on be my partner.'

"The servant with the two thousand showed how he also had doubled his master's investment. His master commended him: 'Good work! You did your job well. From now on be my partner.'

"The servant given one thousand said, 'Master, I know you have high standards and hate careless ways, that you demand the best and make no allowances for error. I was afraid I might disappoint you, so I found a good hiding place and secured your money. Here it is, safe and sound down to the last cent.'

"The master was furious. 'That's a terrible way to live! It's criminal to live cautiously like that! If you knew I was after the best, why did you do less than the least? The least you could have done would have been to invest the sum with the bankers, where at least I would have gotten a little interest.

"'Take the thousand and give it to the one who risked the most. And get rid of this "play-it-safe" who won't go out on a limb. Throw him out into utter darkness.'"

Luke 10:25-37, *the story of the good Samaritan*

Just then a religion scholar stood up with a question to test Jesus. "Teacher, what do I need to do to get eternal life?"

He answered, "What's written in God's Law? How do you interpret it?"

He said, "That you love the Lord your God with all your passion and prayer and muscle and intelligence — and that you love your neighbor as well as you do yourself."

"Good answer!" said Jesus. "Do it and you'll live."

Looking for a loophole, he asked, "And just how would you define 'neighbor'?"

Jesus answered by telling a story. "There was once a man traveling from Jerusalem to Jericho. On the way he was attacked by robbers. They took his clothes, beat him up, and went off leaving him half-dead. Luckily, a priest was on his way down the same road, but when he saw him he angled across to the other side. Then a Levite religious man showed up; he also avoided the injured man.

"A Samaritan traveling the road came on him. When he saw the man's condition, his heart went out to him. He gave him first aid, disinfecting and bandaging his wounds. Then he lifted him onto his donkey, led him to an inn, and made him comfortable. In the morning he took out two silver coins and gave them to the innkeeper, saying, 'Take good care of him. If it costs any more, put it on my bill — I'll pay you on my way back.'

"What do you think? Which of the three became a neighbor to the man attacked by robbers?"

"The one who treated him kindly," the religion scholar responded.

Jesus said, "Go and do the same."

Luke 14:7-14, *the story of a dinner party*

He went on to tell a story to the guests around the table. Noticing how each had tried to elbow into the place of honor, he said, "When someone invites you to dinner, don't take the place of honor. Somebody more important than you might have been invited by the host. Then he'll come and call out in front of everybody, 'You're in the wrong place. The place of honor belongs to this man.' Red-faced, you'll have to make your way to the very last table, the only place left.

"When you're invited to dinner, go and sit at the last place. Then when the host comes he may very well say, 'Friend, come up to the front.' That will give the dinner guests something to talk about! What I'm saying is, If you walk around with your nose in the air, you're going to end up flat on your face. But if you're content to be simply yourself, you will become more than yourself."

Then he turned to the host. "The next time you put on a dinner, don't just invite your friends and family and rich neighbors, the kind of people who will return the favor. Invite some people who never get invited out, the misfits from the wrong side of the tracks. You'll be — and experience — a blessing. They won't be able to return the favor, but the favor will be returned — oh, how it will be returned! — at the resurrection of God's people."

Luke 15:1-7, *the story of the lost sheep*

By this time a lot of men and women of doubtful reputation were hanging around Jesus, listening intently. The Pharisees and religion scholars were not pleased, not at all pleased. They growled, "He takes in sinners and eats meals with them, treating them like old friends." Their grumbling triggered this story.

"Suppose one of you had a hundred sheep and lost one. Wouldn't you leave the ninety-nine in the wilderness and go after the lost one until you found it? When found, you can be sure you would put it across your shoulders, rejoicing, and when you got home call in your friends and neighbors, saying, 'Celebrate with me! I've found my lost sheep!' Count on it — there's more joy in heaven over one sinner's rescued life than over ninety-nine good people in no need of rescue."

Luke 15:8-10, *the story of the lost coin*

> "Or imagine a woman who has ten coins and loses one. Won't she light a lamp and scour the house, looking in every nook and cranny until she finds it? And when she finds it you can be sure she'll call her friends and neighbors: 'Celebrate with me! I found my lost coin!' Count on it — that's the kind of party God's angels throw every time one lost soul turns to God."

Luke 15:11-32, *the story of the lost son*

> Then he said, "There was once a man who had two sons. The younger said to his father, 'Father, I want right now what's coming to me.'
>
> "So the father divided the property between them. It wasn't long before the younger son packed his bags and left for a distant country. There, undisciplined and dissipated, he wasted everything he had. After he had gone through all his money, there was a bad famine all through that country and he began to hurt. He signed on with a citizen there who assigned him to his fields to slop the pigs. He was so hungry he would have eaten the corncobs

in the pig slop, but no one would give him any.

"That brought him to his senses. He said, 'All those farmhands working for my father sit down to three meals a day, and here I am starving to death. I'm going back to my father. I'll say to him, Father, I've sinned against God, I've sinned before you; I don't deserve to be called your son. Take me on as a hired hand.' He got right up and went home to his father.

"When he was still a long way off, his father saw him. His heart pounding, he ran out, embraced him, and kissed him. The son started his speech: 'Father, I've sinned against God, I've sinned before you; I don't deserve to be called your son ever again.'

"But the father wasn't listening. He was calling to the servants, 'Quick. Bring a clean set of clothes and dress him. Put the family ring on his finger and sandals on his feet. Then get a grain-fed heifer and roast it. We're going to feast! We're going to have a wonderful time! My son is here — given up for dead and now alive! Given up for lost and now found!' And they began to have a wonderful time.

"All this time his older son was out in the field. When the day's work was done he came in. As he approached the house, he heard the music and dancing. Calling over one of the houseboys, he asked what was going on. He told him, 'Your brother came home. Your father has ordered a feast — barbecued beef! — because he has him home safe and sound.'

"The older brother stalked off in an angry sulk and refused to join in. His father came out and tried to talk to him, but he wouldn't listen. The son said, 'Look how many years I've stayed here serving you, never giving you one moment of grief, but have you ever thrown a party for me and my friends? Then this son of yours who has thrown away your money on whores shows up and you go all out with a feast!'

"His father said, 'Son, you don't understand. You're with me all the time, and everything that is mine is yours — but this is a wonderful time, and we had to celebrate. This brother of yours was dead, and he's alive! He was lost, and he's found!'"

Luke 18:1-8, *the story of the persistent widow*

Jesus told them a story showing that it was necessary for them to pray consistently and never quit. He said, "There was once a judge in some city who never gave God a thought and cared nothing for people. A widow in that city kept after him: 'My rights are being violated. Protect me!'

"He never gave her the time of day. But after this went on and on he said to himself, 'I care nothing what God thinks, even less what people think. But because this widow won't quit badgering me, I'd better do something and see that she gets justice — otherwise I'm going to end up beaten black and blue by her pounding.'"

Then the Master said, "Do you hear what that judge, corrupt as he is, is saying? So what makes you think God won't step in and work justice for his chosen people, who continue to cry out for help? Won't he stick up for them? I assure you, he will. He will not drag his feet. But how much of that kind of persistent faith will the Son of Man find on the earth when he returns?"

Luke 18:9-17, *the story of the tax man and the Pharisee*

He told his next story to some who were complacently pleased with themselves over their moral performance and looked down their noses at the common people: "Two men went up to the Temple to pray, one a Pharisee, the other a tax man. The Pharisee posed and prayed like this: 'Oh, God, I thank you that I am not like other people—robbers, crooks, adulterers, or, heaven forbid, like this tax man. I fast twice a week and tithe on all my income.'

"Meanwhile the tax man, slumped in the shadows, his face in his hands, not daring to look up, said, 'God, give mercy. Forgive me, a sinner.'"

Jesus commented, "This tax man, not the other, went home made right with God. If you walk around with your nose in the air, you're going to end up flat on your face, but if you're content to be simply yourself, you will become more than yourself."

People brought babies to Jesus, hoping he might touch them. When the disciples saw it, they shooed them off. Jesus called them back. "Let these children alone. Don't get between them and me. These children are the kingdom's pride and joy. Mark this: Unless you accept God's kingdom in the simplicity of a child, you'll never get in."

John 10:1-16, *the story of the good Shepherd*

"Let me set this before you as plainly as I can. If a person climbs over or through the fence of a sheep pen instead of going through the gate, you know he's up to no good — a sheep rustler! The shepherd walks right up to the gate. The gatekeeper opens the gate to him and the sheep recognize his voice. He calls his own sheep by name and leads them out. When he gets them all out, he leads them and they follow because they are familiar with his voice. They won't follow a stranger's voice but will scatter because they aren't used to the sound of it."

Jesus told this simple story, but they had no idea what he was talking about. So he tried again. "I'll be explicit, then. I am the Gate for the sheep. All those others are up to no good — sheep stealers, every one of them. But the sheep didn't listen to them. I am the Gate. Anyone who goes through me will be cared for — will freely go in and out, and find pasture. A thief is only there to steal and kill and destroy. I came so they can have real and eternal life, more and better life than they ever dreamed of.

"I am the Good Shepherd. The Good Shepherd puts the sheep before himself, sacrifices himself if necessary. A hired man is not a real shepherd. The sheep mean nothing to him. He sees a wolf come and runs for it, leaving the sheep to be ravaged and scattered by the wolf. He's only in it for the money. The sheep don't matter to him.

"I am the Good Shepherd. I know my own sheep and my own sheep know me. In the same way, the Father knows me and I know the Father. I put the sheep before myself, sacrificing myself if necessary. You need to know that I have other sheep in addition to those in this pen. I need to gather and bring them, too. They'll also recognize my voice. Then it will be one flock, one Shepherd."

And I'm telling the story of God Eternal,

singing the praises of Jacob's God.

— PSALM 75:9